DESIGN and MAKE

Things to Wear

Margot Richardson

WAYLAND

DESIGN and MAKE

Houses and Homes
Things to Wear
Toys and Games
Wheels and Transport
Simple Machines
Water Projects

First published in 1997 by Wayland Publishers Ltd,
61 Western Road, Hove, East Sussex BN3 1JD, England
© Copyright 1997 Wayland Publishers Ltd
Series planned and produced by Margot Richardson
Find Wayland on the internet at http: //www.wayland.co.uk

British Library Cataloguing in Publication Data
Richardson, Margot
Things to wear. - (Design & make)
1.Decoration and ornament - Juvenile literature
2.Handicraft - Juvenile literature
I.Title
745.5

ISBN 0 7502 2076 7

Commissioned photography by Zul Mukhida
Designed by Tim Mayer
Equipment supplied by Technology Teaching Systems Ltd, Alfreton, UK
Printed and bound in Italy by G. Canale & C.S.p.A., Turin

CONTENTS

Introduction	4
Royal Crown	6
Neck Tie	8
Hair Clips	10
Make Your Own Hat	12
Spectacles	14
Slip-on Shoes	16
Face Mask	18
Necklace	20
Friendship Band	22
Badge with Lights	24
Cloak	26
Carnival Costume	28
Glossary	30
Books to Read	30
Teachers' Notes	31
Index	32

INTRODUCTION

Many thousands of years ago, people started to wear clothes to keep themselves warm. The first clothes were made from animal skins and furs.

Later, about 5,000 years ago, people learned how to make fabric, or cloth. Fabric can be made in many different colours, and people began to make clothes in various shapes.

The types of clothes worn around the world depend a great deal on the climate. People who live in cold countries must wear thick clothes, to keep them warm. People in hot countries wear less, so that they can stay cool.

This picture shows an aboriginal theatre group from northern Australia performing a tribal dance. For special ceremonies, dancers decorate their bodies with paints made from coloured earth.

Of course, we do not wear clothes just for warmth – we like to look attractive, and to wear clothes in styles and colours that suit us. We also choose hair styles and decorate our bodies with make-up and jewellery.

Early people dressed up with necklaces made from shells and seeds, and even painted themselves with colours found in the earth. When metals and jewels were discovered, jewellery became colourful, shiny and highly prized.

People wear different things at different times. Some clothes are worn almost every day. Others are kept for special occasions, such as festivals.

Some of the things we put on our bodies, such as jewellery, are worn just to look interesting.

4

Other things do a particular job. For example, sunglasses screen our eyes from the sun, and scarves keep our necks warm.

Everyone wants the things they wear to look good. But the people who design them have a special job to do. As well as making them look attractive, they must make things work properly. A raincoat needs to be waterproof; a swimming costume should dry quickly; a pair of shoes must be hard-wearing and last for months or even years.

Think about the things you wear each day.

● Write a list of the things you are wearing now.

● What are they made from?

● What different things do you wear when you go somewhere special, for example, to a party?

Things that are worn include clothes, shoes, jewellery and make-up. We often decide what people are like from the way they look.

Lapp people live in northern Norway, where there is often snow all year round. These traditional clothes were designed to keep out the cold.

ROYAL CROWN

YOU WILL NEED

Gold cardboard

Large coloured beads that look like jewels

Fake fur (optional)

Two stick-on touch-and-close fastener dots (eg Velcro)

Large sheet of paper

Tape measure

PVA glue

Pencil

Ruler

Scissors

For hundreds of years, the kings and queens of Europe have worn a crown on special occasions. A crown shows that they are the most important person in their country.

Here is a crown you can make out of simple materials. Use it for a school play, or a history project.

1 Work out how big the crown has to be. Measure round your head, just above the ears, with a tape measure. Add 5cm to this length.

2 Cut out a piece of paper, to make a template for the crown. It should be the length worked out in step 1, and about 20cm wide.

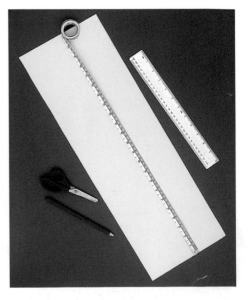

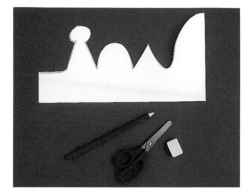

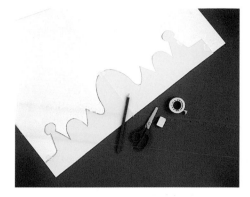

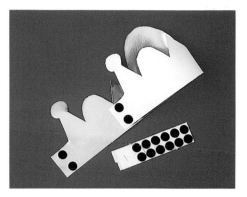

3 Fold the piece of paper in half. Draw the shape of the crown on one side of the paper. When you are happy with the shape, cut it out.

4 Unfold the paper template and put it on the plain side of the gold cardboard. Draw around the shape. Cut the shape out of the cardboard.

5 Put the stick-on fastener dots at either end of the crown, about 1.5cm in from the edge. The hard dots should go on the gold side. Stick the soft dots on the plain side.

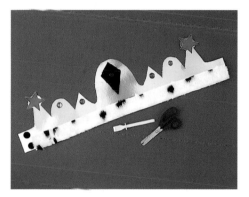

6 Decorate the crown. Glue on beads to look like jewels. You can also stick on fake fur along the bottom edge.

Queen Elizabeth II wears a crown on important days, such as the State Opening of the British Parliament. This crown is made from gold, which is very heavy. It is decorated with some of the biggest gems in the world. The fur at the bottom makes it more comfortable to wear.

7

NECK TIE

YOU WILL NEED

Scraps of fabric, preferably crisp cotton

● Dressmaking elastic, approx 1cm wide x 40cm long

3 small safety pins

Tape measure

Pencil

Ruler

Scissors

Neck ties are mainly worn by men. They are called ties because they are tied round the neck with special knots. Here is a way of making one that is easier to put on.

Before you start, make sure the fabric does not have any creases in it. Ask an adult to iron it for you, if necessary.

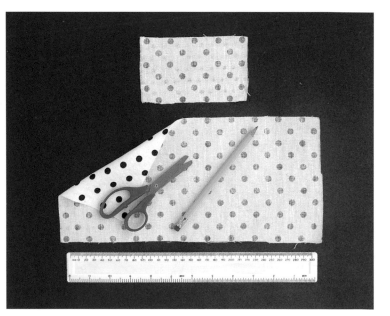

1 Draw two rectangles on the wrong side of the fabric. One piece should be about 32 x 15cm. The other should measure about 13 x 7.5 cm. Cut them out.

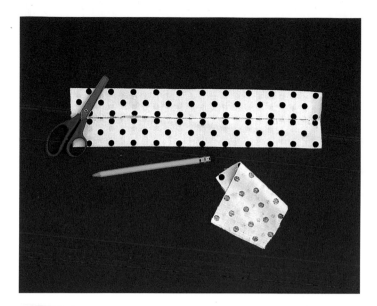

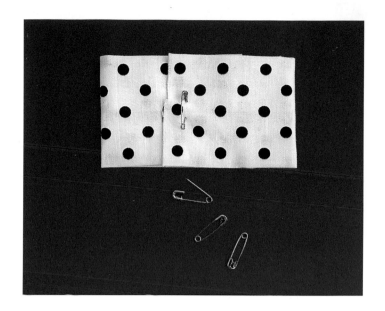

2 Fold the larger piece of fabric lengthways, turning both the long edges into the centre. Make creases along the folds by pressing them with your fingertips.

3 Fold this piece of fabric again but in the other direction, so that it overlaps at the back by about 5cm. Hold it in place with a safety pin.

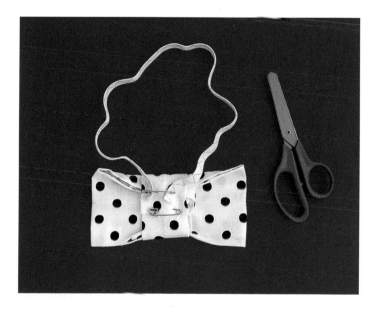

4 Fold the smaller piece of fabric in the same way as step 2. Then fold it round the larger piece at right angles, to make the bow shape. Use another safety pin to hold it.

5 Take the piece of elastic. Pin both ends to the back of the bow tie. Put the tie on to see if the elastic is too long or too short. Change the length of the elastic if necessary.

NOW TRY THIS

Make some more ties that are different shapes. Try a long thin office-tie shape, or a much bigger, floppier bow tie.

HAIR CLIPS

YOU WILL NEED

- Metal hair clips
- Materials for decoration such as ribbon, fabric, felt, cardboard, beads, pasta shapes, fake flowers, etc.
- Masking tape
- PVA glue
- Plastic modelling clay (eg Plasticine)
- Pencil
- Ruler
- Scissors
- Paints (optional)

People all round the world enjoy arranging and decorating their hair. This can vary from putting flowers in it, to fancy hair styles.

Here is a way of decorating clips to wear in your hair. Use your imagination when choosing the decoration, but remember to keep the objects as light as possible.

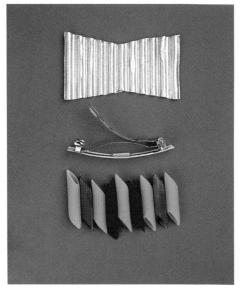

1 Cover the bar of the metal hair clip with a length of masking tape. Make sure the tape is stuck on securely.

2 Measure the length and the width of the bar, and make sure that the planned decoration will cover it properly – so that no masking tape is left showing round the edges.

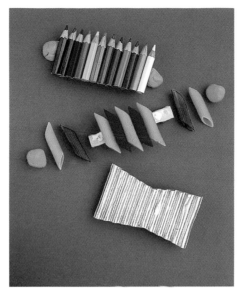

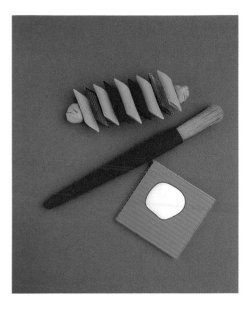

3 Put a coat of PVA glue on the masking tape. Let it dry a little, until it feels sticky.

4 Press the decoration on to the glued surface, and let the glue dry. If necessary, use a few pieces of modelling clay to hold things in place until the glue dries.

5 Painting some types of decoration with a coat of PVA will make them harder and stronger. This will make them last longer.

Beautiful hair styles are an important part of a Japanese woman's traditional dress.

MAKE YOUR OWN HAT

Hats are worn for a number of reasons. In hot countries they are used to shade faces from the sun. They are also useful to keep our heads dry when it rains, and to make sure they stay warm during a cold winter. Sometimes a hat can show how important someone is.

Hats can be many different shapes, and made out of all sorts of materials. Some hats are hard and others are soft.

YOU WILL NEED

- Large sheet of thin cardboard
- Fabric, or felt, for covering
- Decoration such as wool, ribbon, tassel, etc. (optional)
- Masking tape
- PVA glue
- Tape measure
- Pencil
- Ruler
- Scissors

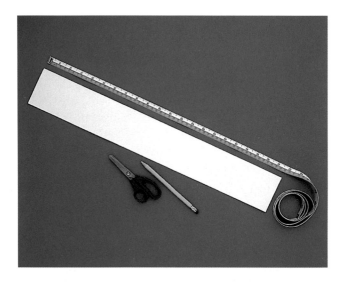

1 Measure round your head with the tape measure, just above the ears. On a piece of thin card, draw a long rectangle. It should be the length above, plus another 2cm, and about 7.5cm wide.

2 Cut out the rectangle. Bend it into a circle and join it at the short ends with masking tape. The ends should overlap a little. Put the circle on your head to see if it fits.

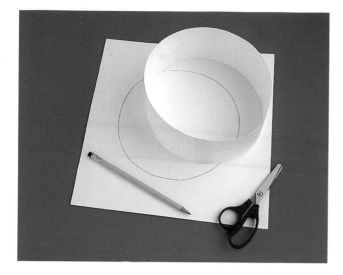

3 Stand this circle on a piece of thin card. Draw round the circle, taking care not to push it it out of shape. Cut out the flat disc. This will form a template for the top of the hat.

4 Undo the cardboard circle. Use the cardboard pieces as templates, to draw the same two shapes on the fabric or felt. Then cut them out

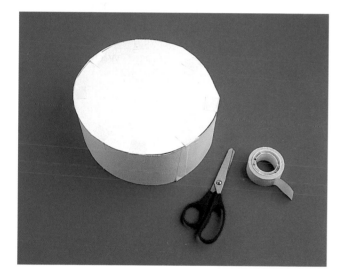

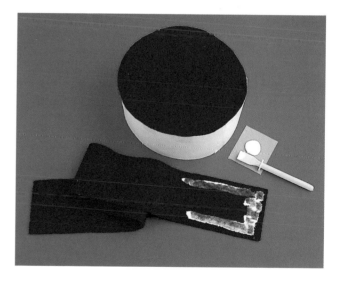

5 Make the hat shape in the cardboard. Rejoin the ends of the long rectangle, as in step 2. Then stick the top of the hat to the sides with small pieces of masking tape.

6 When the cardboard shape is finished, glue the fabric pieces to the card. Make sure there is no white cardboard showing. You may like to add decorations, such as a tassel on top, or a coloured band around the side.

NOW TRY THIS

Once you have made a basic hat, add a brim. Put the finished hat on a large piece of cardboard, draw round it carefully, then draw a larger circle round the first one. Cut out the card ring and tape it to the lower edge of the hat. Cover it in fabric, as in step 6.

SPECTACLES

Some people cannot see as well as others. They wear spectacles, or glasses, with special lenses to improve their eyesight. People also wear sunglasses, with coloured lenses, to shade their eyes from bright sunlight.

The spectacles shown here do not work like real glasses, but show you a way of making a frame with hinges.

WARNING!

These glasses will not protect your eyes from the sun. Do not wear them for long periods, and *never* look directly at the sun.

YOU WILL NEED

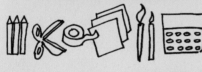

Cardboard, two different types or colours

Coloured plastic or acetate sheets

Plain paper

Masking tape

Pencil

Ruler

Scissors

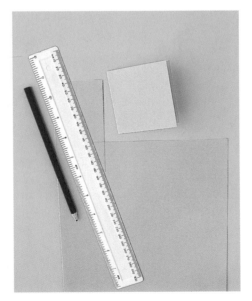

1 Draw a rectangle on a piece of paper. It should be about 15cm long, and 5 to 7.5cm wide. Cut it out and fold it in half.

2 Draw the shape of one side of the spectacles on the paper. Remember to make a space for the nose. Cut out the shape, through both thicknesses of the paper to make a shape that is symmetrical (the same on either side).

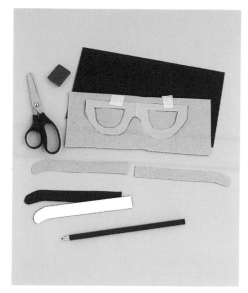

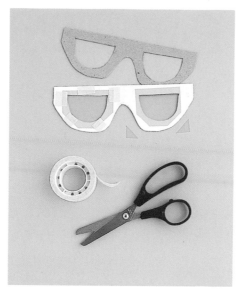

3 Use the paper template to draw the frame shape on two different types of cardboard. Also cut out two arms, again in the two types of card. The arms must be mirror images of each other.

4 Cut pieces of coloured plastic or acetate to make the 'lenses'. They should be slightly larger than the holes to be covered. Stick them onto the wrong side of the cardboard with small pieces of masking tape.

5 Join the arms to the frames with pieces of masking tape, to make hinges. Make sure the hinges can bend freely.

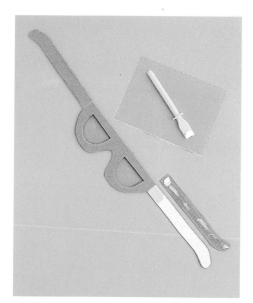

Sunglasses have dark lenses to shade eyes from the sun. Although the name makes them sound as though they are made from glass, many spectacles are now made from plastic.

6 Glue the two frames to each other, with their wrong sides together. The plastic lenses should be sandwiched in the middle of the finished frame.

NOW TRY THIS

Now that you have made some basic spectacles, design some shapes that are more interesting. They could be square, round or oval. Decorate the front of the frame with paints, or glue on glitter or beads.

SLIP-ON SHOES

YOU WILL NEED

- Thick corrugated cardboard, from a carton or box
- Coloured paper or fabric
- Thin cardboard
- Sticky-backed plastic
- PVA glue
- Sticky or masking tape
- Tape measure
- Pencil
- Scissors

Shoes protect our feet. They let us walk over rough ground without it hurting, and they keep our feet warm when it is cold.

But shoes can do all sorts of other jobs too. Think of the difference between slippers worn by a ballerina and the boots worn by a worker on a building site. Some shoes can be very plain, while others are brightly coloured and decorated.

1 Put your foot on a piece of thin card and draw round it with a pencil. Do the same for the other foot. Then cut out the foot shapes.

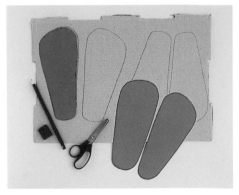

2 Put the foot templates on the thick cardboard and mark out two pieces for each foot. Mark them Left and Right and cut them out. Cut another left and right shape from coloured paper or fabric.

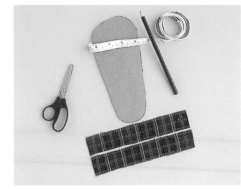

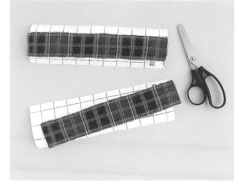

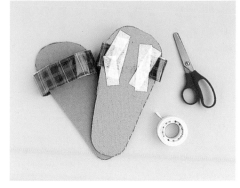

3 Measure round the widest part of your foot with a tape measure. Add on an extra 5cm. Cut out two pieces of coloured paper, or fabric. They should be the length above, and about 3 to 4cm wide.

4 Cut two pieces of sticky-backed plastic, the same length as in step 3, but much wider. Peel off the paper backing and put the coloured paper or fabric in the centre of the sticky side of the plastic. Fold over the edges and stick them down.

5 Put one of the plastic-covered strips over the widest part of a cardboard 'foot'. It should overlap each side by about 2.5cm. Stick it in place underneath with the sticky or masking tape.

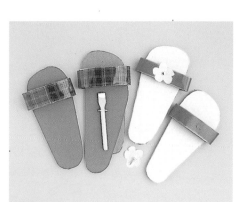

6 Glue the matching cardboard shape to the underside of the shoe. Make sure the ends of the plastic-covered strip are stuck neatly between the two layers.

7 Glue the coloured foot shape to the top surface of the shoe. If you wish, add some extra decoration to the top of the shoe.

NOW TRY THIS

Design another pair of shoes, with a different shape that covers the foot. You could add a strap to go round the back of your heel. Experiment to find the best way of fixing this to the piece at the front.

Shoes are most often made in factories, but this shoemaker in Pakistan makes and sells shoes in a small shop.

FACE MASK

YOU WILL NEED

- Thin cardboard
- Plain paper
- Scraps of coloured paper, egg cartons, fabric, etc. for shapes and decoration
- 5mm-wide elastic, approx 30cm long
- Two metal paper fasteners
- PVA glue
- Masking tape
- Pencil
- Ruler
- Scissors
- Paints (optional)

A mask is a covering that hides a person's face. Masks have been worn by different peoples around the world, for many thousands of years.

Some masks are for safety, such as masks worn by doctors, or by catchers in baseball. Others are worn at parties or festivals, by actors in the theatre, or for special ceremonies.

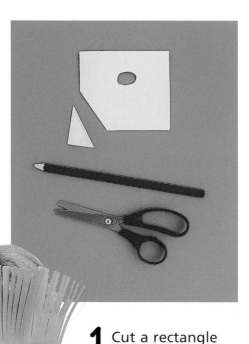

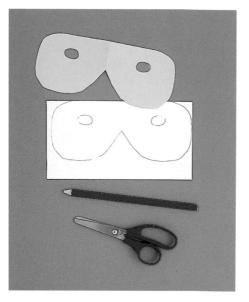

1 Cut a rectangle of paper, approximately 18 x 8cm. Fold it in half and cut an upside-down V in the centre. Also cut holes to see through.

2 Try the paper over your face to see if it fits. Change the shape if necessary. Use it as a template and cut the shape out of thin card.

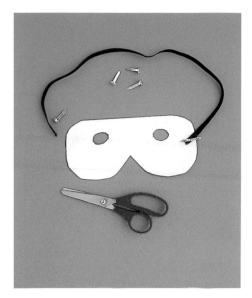

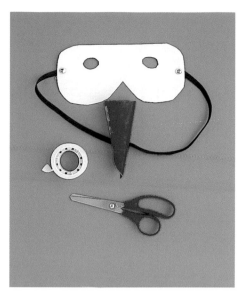

3 Fasten the elastic on one side with a paper fastener. Hold the mask on your face and work out how much elastic is needed round the back of your head to hold the mask on firmly. Join the elastic to the other side with another paper fastener.

4 Add a nose to the mask. It could be made from part of an egg carton, or a piece of rolled or folded cardboard. Stick it on with masking tape. Check that the nose piece fits over your nose.

5 Add something to the top of the mask to hide your hair. It could be made from paper or fabric. Tape or glue it to the top of the eye covering.

6 You may wish to add a lower piece to the mask, to cover the rest of your face. Use your imagination to make it look as different as possible from the way your face normally looks.

A large mask can completely change the way a person looks, making them like an animal or a monster. This mask comes from Matabeleland, in Zimbabwe.

NECKLACE

YOU WILL NEED

- Coloured wrapping paper
- Short piece of wooden dowel, about 5mm diameter
- Coloured embroidery thread
- Coloured beads (optional)
- Vaseline/petroleum jelly
- PVA glue
- Pencil
- Ruler
- Scissors

A necklace is a type of jewellery. Necklaces can be made out of many things, from leaves and flowers to precious gems such as diamonds.

Here is a way of making your own necklace, from beads made out of nothing more than a piece of coloured paper.

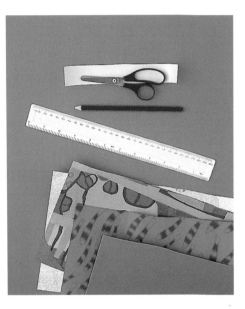

1 Decide on the length of your necklace. Put a piece of embroidery thread around a friend's neck and work out what length looks best. Take the thread off, add about 2.5cm (to allow for a knot) and cut it.

2 Decide on the width of the beads. They can be anything from about 1cm to 4cm. Turn the paper over so that it is plain side up. Measure out a long strip, 1–4cm wide, and at least 20cm long.

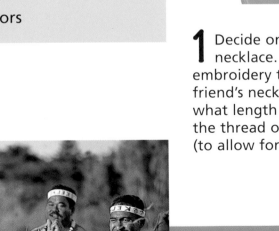

In some countries jewellery is worn just by women, but in others, both men and women decorate their bodies in this way. These dancers from Tokelau, tiny islands in the middle of the Pacific Ocean, wear shell necklaces.

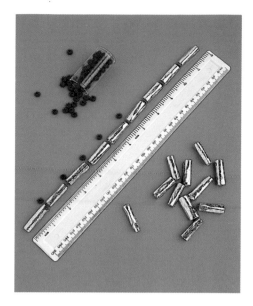

3 Rub some Vaseline on one end of the wooden dowel. Cover the wrong (plain) side of the paper with plenty of glue.

4 Place the dowel right at one end of the glued paper. Roll the paper round the dowel, as tightly as possible. Keep rolling up the paper to make a neat bead shape. Take out the dowel. Put the bead aside to dry.

5 If you are happy with the size and shape of your bead, work out how many you will need to complete your necklace. Cut enough strips of paper to make all the beads, and roll them up as in step 4.

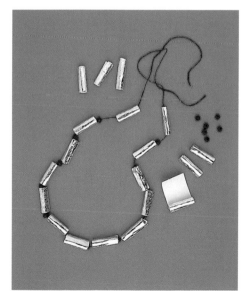

6 Thread the beads on to the embroidery thread. You can use bought beads to add to the necklace, if you wish. When all the beads are threaded, tie the ends of the thread together neatly.

NOW TRY THIS

● **Instead of using long rectangles of paper, try making beads from long triangles. Experiment with different lengths and widths to make a variety of shapes.**

● **Make beads from plain paper and paint them after they have been made. When the paint is dry, 'varnish' them with a coat of PVA glue.**

FRIENDSHIP BAND

Make a colourful band and give it to a good friend. These bands are usually made from knotted cotton, but here is another way to make them, and learn about weaving at the same time.

YOU WILL NEED

- Wool (or thick cotton) in a variety of colours
- Stiff cardboard, approx 20 x 15cm
- Piece of stiff cardboard, approx 15 x 3cm
- Large, blunt darning needle
- Sticky tape
- Pencil
- Ruler
- Scissors

1 Take the large piece of card. At each short end, in the middle, make ten small cuts, about 2mm apart. Make sure the cuts are exactly opposite each other.

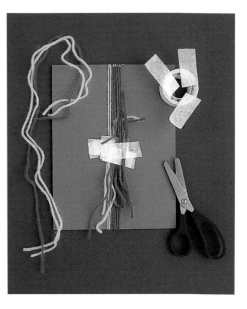

2 Cut ten lengths of wool in different colours, about 40cm long. Stretch them between the notches in the card, and fix them tightly in position at the back, with tape.

Some ways of weaving fabric are very simple. All that is needed is to stretch out the long threads to weave across. This African man is weaving outdoors. He has stretched his threads between some small trees.

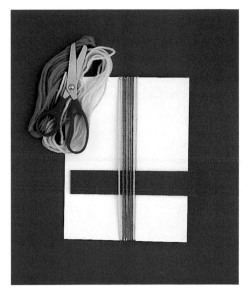

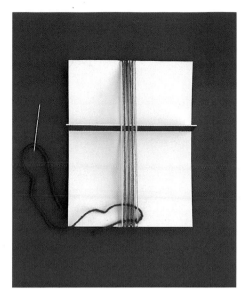

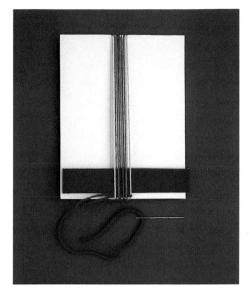

3 Take the long thin piece of card. Pass it under the first length of wool, over the second, under the third, over the fourth, etc, until you reach the other side.

4 Cut a long length of wool. Thread one end through the needle. Tie the other end to a thread at the bottom. Turn the thin card on its side, and feed both ends of the wool through from one side to the other.

5 Pull the wool tight. Then turn the card so that it is flat again, and use it to push the weaving down to the bottom. Push the card back up and leave it where it is.

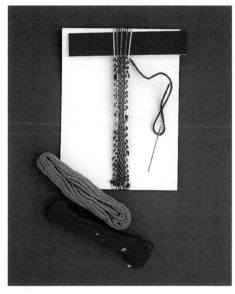

6 Using the needle, weave it through the wool so that it goes <u>over</u> the first length of wool, <u>under</u> the second, <u>over</u> the third, etc, until you reach the other side. Pull the wool through and use the card to push the weaving down.

7 Continue in this way, changing colours as you wish until you are about 5cm from the top of the card. Carefully remove the wool from the card, knot the ends so they will not come undone, and your band is ready to tie round your wrist.

BADGE WITH LIGHTS

YOU WILL NEED

- Piece of thick, lightweight card, such as foam board
- One or two 2-volt flashing LEDs, 5mm diameter
- Battery (4.5V minimum)
- 1.2m approx single core electric wire
- Wire cutter and stripper
- Large safety pin
- Masking tape
- Hole punch, same diameter as LED
- Pencil
- Craft knife and steel rule (optional)
- Scissors

Here is a way of using a small electrical current and flashing lights to make a badge that is unusual and fun. The lights, called LEDs, are joined with wire to a battery. Pin the badge to your clothes, with the battery hidden in your pocket.

Design it to look like anything you like, such as a scary face, a spider, an animal or even a truck with headlights.

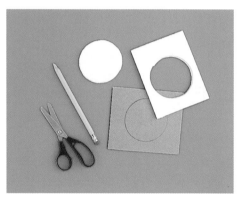

1 Draw the shape of the badge on the card. Cut it out with scissors or get an adult to help you with a craft knife.

2 Mark where the LED is to go. Punch a hole in the card. Push the LED through the hole and flatten its wire legs on to the card.

A badge usually tells us something about the person who is wearing it. It may give the person's name, or show that he or she belongs to a club. Sometimes a badge shows someone's job, or how old they are. Other badges have a message on them, or just a bright picture.

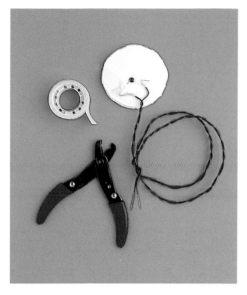

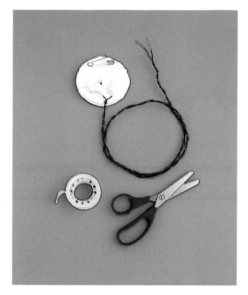

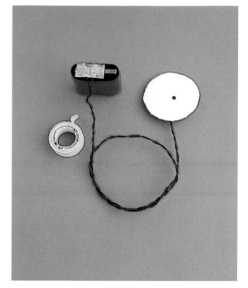

3 Cut two lengths of wire about 60cm long. Strip about 2cm of the plastic covering from each end of the wires. Join an end to each leg of the LED. Twist the wires together all the way down their length.

4 Stick the safety pin to the back of the badge with several pieces of masking tape. Make sure the pin side is facing outwards.

5 You will need to attach the other end of each wire to a battery terminal. Use masking tape to keep the wires in place. If the LED does not work, swap the ends over to the other terminals.

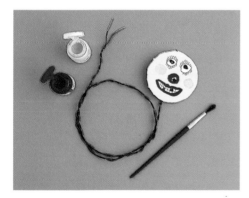

6 Decorate the badge, making sure that the LED is part of your design. When the paint is dry, pin the badge to your shirt, feed the wires down inside, and attach them to the battery.

A craft knife can be dangerous if it is not used properly. Always ask an adult to help you use one.

● **To avoid accidents, never play with sharp knives.**

● **If possible, use a steel rule to guide the knife.**

CLOAK

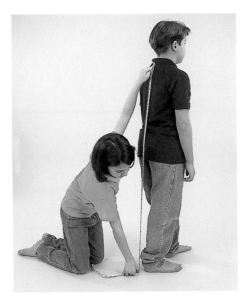

1 Measure the person who is going to wear the cloak. Find the length from the back of their neck, to just above the floor.

2 Also, with their arms outstretched, measure the width from one wrist, across their back, to the other wrist.

3 Make a paper pattern for the cloak. It should be the same length as step 1, and half the width measured in step 2. Make the bottom curved at one corner. Cut out the pattern. Hold it up against the person to make sure it is the correct size.

YOU WILL NEED

- Fabric (see Steps 1 and 2 for measurements)
- Five stick-on touch-and-close fastener dots (eg Velcro)
- Large sheet of paper, such as brown paper
- Long sleeved shirt
- Tape measure
- Pencil
- Scissors

Many years ago, cloaks were often worn instead of overcoats. A cloak can be fun to wear as it swirls about or floats behind the person wearing it.

To make this cloak, it is important to measure the person who will be wearing it. It is joined to their shirt with touch-and-close fasteners.

4 Fold the fabric in half and lay it out flat on the floor. Put the paper pattern on top of it. Make sure the long, centre edge is right against the fold. Draw round the edges with pencil or felt-tip pen. Cut out the fabric.

5 Open out the fabric and lay it flat. Stick fastener dots along the top edge. Space them evenly. Make sure they are on the wrong side of the fabric.

6 Put the other halves of the fastener dots along the arms and neck of a long-sleeved shirt. They should also be the same distance apart as on the cloak.

7 Put on the long-sleeved shirt. Press the two rows of dots together – and the cloak is finished.

This cloak is worn by a Native American. It is decorated with a crow made from red fabric and buttons sewn on.

NOW TRY THIS

Once you have seen how this cloak is made, design another with a more interesting shape. It could have pleats at the top, or a jagged lower edge, like a bat's wings.

CARNIVAL COSTUME

YOU WILL NEED

- Recycled cardboard boxes
- Cotton tape, approx 5cm wide and 60cm long
- Large metal paper fasteners
- Thick cardboard (for head piece, optional)
- Wood, approx 1 x 1cm square (optional)
- Various papers such as brown, crepe, tissue and/or newspaper
- Paints and brushes (optional)
- Masking or sticky tape
- PVA glue
- Scissors
- Pencil
- Plain paper for drawing

Carnivals are like big parties, and are usually held outdoors. In the big, famous carnivals, such as the one in Rio de Janeiro, Brazil, people dress up in fantastic costumes that can take many months to make.

Use your imagination to design your own costume, made out of recycled materials. It could be anything from an animal to a rocket, a robot to a skeleton. Draw a picture of how you would like your costume to look.

1 Find a cardboard box that will go around the top part of your body. Cut off, or fold out, the top and the bottom, and try it on to make sure it fits round you.

2 Hang the box from your shoulders using wide cotton tape, fixed at either end with the large metal paper fasteners. Cut holes at either side for your arms.

Some carnival costumes have big frames which are decorated with all sorts of materials in bright colours. The costumes are supported on people's shoulders. The wearers have to keep the costume on as they dance around the streets.

3 Add extra shapes to the box. You can make them in all sorts of different ways. For example, cut them out of thick cardboard from old boxes. Make joints that move, using metal paper fasteners. Or use paper or fabric joined with masking or sticky tape.

4 Put a head piece on the costume. It can be taller than the top of your head. Use masking tape to join some thick card, (or 1 x 1cm wood), to the box to hold up the shape. Remember to make eye holes so that you can see out.

5 Decorate the entire costume by using coloured paper, or painting the paper and card. Don't forget to make your legs and arms part of the costume. Let the paint and any glue dry before wearing it.

GLOSSARY

brim	The edge of a hat that sticks out.
ceremony	A way of doing things on a special occasion, such as when people get married, or when dead people are buried.
crease	A line made by folding or wrinkles. Creases can be made in paper, card and fabric.
diameter	The distance across the centre of a circle, from one side to the other.
disc	A shape that is round and flat. An example is a compact disc (CD).
fabric	Material that has been woven or knitted, from cotton or wool, for example.
fake	Something that pretends to be something else, that is not real.
frame	A strong shape that can hold up things stuck to it.
gem	A precious stone that has been cut and polished, such as a diamond, emerald or ruby.
hinge	A joint that moves, letting things joined to it go backwards and forwards.
jewellery	Gems or ornaments worn on a person's body.
LED	Short for Light-Emitting Diode. An LED is like a tiny light bulb.
lens	A piece of glass or plastic that is curved on one or both sides. The curve bends rays of light.
mirror image	The opposite of a shape, as though it has been reflected in a mirror.
pattern	Pieces of paper that show how to cut out fabric for clothes or decoration that is put onto paper or fabric.
pleat	Two folds that are placed on top of each other, usually in clothes.
rectangle	A shape with four sides, where two opposite sides of the same length are longer than the other two sides.
recycled	Using something again that has already been used before.
symmetrical	A shape that can be divided down the middle and is exactly the same on either side.
template	A shape used to draw around and cut out a number of pieces that are the same.
terminal	The parts of a battery where other things – such as wires – can be joined to it.
traditional	Something that has been done or used for hundreds of years.
weaving	Making flat fabric by lacing together long threads running in two directions.
wrong side	The side of paper, card or fabric that does not have colour or a pattern on it.

BOOKS TO READ

Arts and Crafts: Weaving by Susie O'Reilly and Zul Mukhida, Wayland, 1993

Clothes in Hot and Cold Places by Simon Crisp, Wayland, 1994

Eyewitness Guides: Costume by L Rowland-Warne, Dorling Kindersley, 1992

Exploring Technology: Textiles by Susie O'Reilly and Jenny Hughes, Wayland, 1991

Festivals: Carnival by Clare Chandler, Wayland, 1997

On Your Feet! by Karin Luisa Batt, Children's Press (Chicago) 1994

Traditions Around the World: Masks by Amanda Earl and Danielle Sensier, Wayland 1994

Traditions Around the World: Jewellery and Accessories by Louise Tythacott, Wayland 1994

TEACHERS' NOTES

Most primary-age children have yet to develop the concept of design, and have had little experience of the materials and techniques needed to make items that function well. However, all children have first-hand knowledge of wearing clothes, hats and shoes, etc., so the topic of Things to Wear gives them plenty of opportunity to use their own experience as a starting point when considering design and manufacture.

Few children of the target age group (seven to nine year olds) are able to sew competently, whether by hand or machine, so this book has been specifically developed to use alternative construction techniques that are within children's capabilities.

Royal Crown While children should be allowed as much freedom as possible to make imaginative designs they can also be encouraged to research and examine 'real' examples. This provides excellent opportunities to link with cross-curricular topics in drama and history. The touch-and-close (Velcro) fastener system allows the size to be somewhat flexible, and could stimulate discussion on size and fitting.

Neck Tie This method allows children to create an item out of fabric, but without a stitch of sewing. A crisp cotton that creases easily under pressure from the fingertips is ideal. To avoid distortion when creasing, the fabric must be cut on the straight grain (ie parallel to the direction of the fibres). It is a good opportunity to examine the 'right' and 'wrong' sides of printed fabric, and could lead to, or even utilize, craft-linked exercises in simple printing techniques. Again, fitting is introduced by the necessary adjustment of the length of elastic around the neck.

Hair Clips Materials for decoration must be chosen carefully to ensure that they will adhere to the masking tape surface using just PVA glue. Durability is addressed in step 5, and children could experiment with different materials, evaluating performance over time.

Make Your Own Hat Measuring the head and getting the hat to fit is of paramount importance for a successful result. Although somewhat similar to the crown project the method of construction requires greater precision and skill. Once children have grasped the basic principles, they should be encouraged to experiment with a variety of different shapes.

Spectacles An ideal opportunity to explain symmetry. Some confusion may arise at first between one shape being symmetrical and two shapes being mirror images of each other. (The latter is essential if arm pieces are to be cut from cardboard that is coloured on one side only.) There is also an ideal opportunity to examine hinges and where they are used – not just on the spectacles themselves.

Slip-on Shoes Tracing around and comparing foot shapes will help children understand the need for different sizes of footwear. The band across the foot is covered in plastic for reinforcement. It may be useful to guide children through experimentation with various materials for this band, to open the way for discussion on both comfort and durability.

Face Mask Another opportunity to link technology with cross-curricular topics such as geography and other cultures. It may be helpful to use sticky tape to cover the legs of the paper fasteners, once joined, to avoid scratches on children's faces. Face masks may be usefully linked with the Carnival Costume activity.

Necklace Measurement is an essential part of this project, both in establishing the finished length of the necklace, and by dividing this by the width of the beads to calculate the number needed.

Friendship Band This teaches the basic principles of weaving to produce a result that children will find appealing. Some children may need help to thread the needle, by twisting the yarn into a tight spiral loop before pushing it firmly into the needle's eye.

Badge with Lights This uses a simple electrical circuit to enliven a straightforward project. Flashing LEDs are available from high-street electronic suppliers in a variety of colours. The correct connection to the battery is easily found by experimentation, as explained in the steps.

Cloak Measuring is the most important facet of this project. Take care to use the correct variety of touch-and-close fastener: those that are sufficiently sticky and do not require sewing in place. Lightweight fabric is also advisable.

Carnival Costume An opportunity for children to indulge creative talents to the full, building on the basic structure explained in the steps, using a variety of materials in an imaginative way. Encourage children to make preliminary drawings, and to explore how they will translate their ideas into three-dimensional shapes. It is important for them to remember that the costume must allow movement of both arms and legs, and some vision, at least to the front.

INDEX

Badge with Lights 24–25
badges 24

Carnival Costume 28–29
ceremonies 18, 30
climate 4–5
Cloak 26–27
clothes 4–5, 26–27
crowns 4, 5

elastic 8–9, 18–19
electricity 24–25

fabric 4, 8–9, 12–13, 16, 22, 26–27, 30
Face Mask 18–19
festivals 4
Friendship Band 22–23
fur 4, 6–7

gems 4, 6–7

Hair Clips 10–11
hair styles 4, 5, 11
hats 12
hinges 15, 30

jewellery 4, 5, 20–21

knots 8, 23

LEDs 24–25, 30
lenses 14, 15

Make Your Own Hat 12
masks 18, 19

Necklace 20–21
Neck Tie 8–9

plastic 15, 16–17

Royal Crown 6–7

shoes 4, 5, 16, 17
Slip-on Shoes 16–17
Spectacles 14–15
sunglasses 4, 14, 15

weaving 22–23, 30

Acknowledgements

The author and publishers wish to thank the following for their kind assistance with this book: models Josie Kearns, Yasmin Mukhida, Charlotte Page, Tom Rigby and Ranga Silva. Also Gabriella Casemore, Zul Mukhida, Philippa Smith and Gus Ferguson.

For the use of their library photographs, grateful thanks are due to: Bryan and Cherry Alexander p5 (bottom); Eye Ubiquitous p11 (Frank Leather), p20 (Matthew McKee), p28–29 (David Cumming); James Davis Travel Photography, p4, p19; Popperfoto/John Stillwell p7; Zul/Chapel Studios p5 top (Graham Horner), p15, p27.
All other photographs belong to the Wayland Picture Library: p12, p17 (Jimmy Holmes), p22, p24.